BRITISH RAILWAYS STEAMING ON THE LONDON MIDLAND REGION

Volume One

Compiled by
PETER HANDS & COLIN RICHARDS

DEFIANT PUBLICATIONS
190 Yoxall Road, Shirley
Solihull, West Midlands.

Printed in the United Kingdom by Netherwood Dalton & Co Ltd, Huddersfield, England.

ACKNOWLEDGEMENTS

Grateful thanks are extended to the following contributors of photographs not only for their use in this book but for their kind patience and long term loan of negatives/photographs whilst this book was being compiled.

K. BARROW BLETCHLEY	G. S. BIRTWELL STANDISH	H. H. BLEADS BIRMINGHAM
L. BROWNHILL BRIERLEY HILL	P. CANE HATFIELD	R. S. CARPENTER BIRMINGHAM
R. A. DANES BROMSGROVE	E. A. ELIAS WOLVERHAMPTON	P. GARDNER NORBURY
J. D. GOMERSALL SHEFFIELD	PETER HAY HOVE	R. HENNEFER SUTTON COLDFIELD
R. W. HINTON GLOUCESTER	C. HUGHES AMESBURY	D. K. JONES MOUNTAIN ASH
M. JOYCE HITCHIN	B. J. MILLER BARRY	MICHAEL PAINE KIDDERMINSTER
R. PICTON WOLVERHAMPTON	W. G. PIGGOTT HADDENHAM	N. E. PREEDY HUCCLECOTE
B. G. PRICE WOLVERHAMPTON	B. RANDS WESTON-SUPER-MARE	K. L. SEAL ANDOVERSFORD
G. W. SHARPE BARNSLEY	M. P. SMITH TORRINGTON	C. P. STACEY STONY STRATFORD
M. S. STOKES MARPLE	D. TITHERIDGE FAREHAM	A. WAKEFIELD DRONFIELD
T. WALTON COVENTRY	TERRY WARD NORTHAMPTON	T. WRIGHT SLOUGH

Other photograph albums which are available are as follows:

BRITISH RAILWAYS STEAMING THROUGH THE SIXTIES – Volumes One to Four

BRITISH RAILWAYS STEAMING ON THE WESTERN REGION – Volume One.

Other titles available from Defiant Publications.

WHAT HAPPENED TO STEAM – Volumes 1 to 50.

CHASING STEAM ON SHED

BR STEAM SHED ALLOCATIONS – Parts 1 to 3. Western Region sheds 81A-89C.

Front Cover – Jubilee Class 4-6-0 No 45563 *Australia* passes Hatch End with a down fitted freight in the mid-afternoon of 27th June 1964. Many road bridges had to be rebuilt to accommodate the overhead catenary and the one at Hatch End had recently been finished. (M. S. Stokes)

ISBN 0 946857 05 9   (C) P. B. HANDS/C. RICHARDS 1985

INTRODUCTION

BRITISH RAILWAYS STEAMING ON THE LONDON MIDLAND REGION –
Volume One is the second book from the 'British Railways Steaming Through the Sixties' stable to be published which concentrates solely on an individual region of British Railways.

These books are designed to give the ordinary, everyday steam photographic enthusiast of the 1950's and 1960's a chance to participate in and give pleasure to others whilst recapturing the twilight days of steam.

Apart from the main series, further individual regional albums will be produced from time to time. Wherever possible, no famous names will be found but the content and quality of the majority of photographs used will be second to none.

BRITISH RAILWAYS STEAMING ON THE LONDON MIDLAND REGION – Volume One takes the reader on a nostalgic journey in excess of 400 miles along the West Coast Main Line through England & Scotland from London (Euston) – Glasgow (Central) via Northampton and Birmingham. Unless otherwise stated, all locomotives are of LMS origin.

In this particular album it has obviously not been possible to include all of the locations on this journey but with one or two exceptions all relevant steam sheds have been included. Some areas of greater interest e.g. Crewe have been given more coverage than others.

The London Midland Region of British Railways had the largest numbers of steam locomotives including the mighty *Coronation* and *Princess* classes of Pacifics. The authors have tried to present a wide selection of locations and locomotive classes from the London Midland & Scottish Regions in an effort to make this album as balanced and as interesting as possible.

The majority of the photographs used in this album have been contributed by readers of Peter Hands series of booklets entitled ''What Happened to Steam'' and from readers of the ''BR Steaming Through the Sixties'' albums. In normal circumstances these may have been hidden from the public eye for ever.

The continuation of the 'BR Steaming' series depends upon you the reader. If you feel you have suitable material of BR steam locomotives and wish to contribute them towards the series and other future publications please contact either:

Peter Hands,
190 Yoxall Road,
Shirley, Solihull,
West Midlands B90 3RN.

OR

Colin Richards,
28 Kendrick Close,
Damson Parkway, Solihull,
West Midlands B92 0QD.

CONTENTS

NAMEPLATES – Some example nameplates of LMS locomotives.

1) Unrebuilt *Patriot* Class 4-6-0 No 45509 *The Derbyshire Yeomanry*. (A. Wakefield)

2) *Jubilee* Class 4-6-0 No 45595 *Southern Rhodesia*. (A. Wakefield)

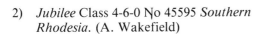

3) *Royal Scot* Class 4-6-0 No 46121 *Highland Light Infantry the City of Glasgow Regiment*. (A. Wakefield)

4) *Princess* Class 4-6-2 No 46202 *Princess Anne*. (A. Wakefield)

5) *Coronation* Class 4-6-2 No 46253 *City of St. Albans*. (A. Wakefield)

6) Our northbound journey commences at London (Euston) which has been completely rebuilt since these photographs were taken. 1A Willesden based *Jubilee* Class 4-6-0 No 45624 *St. Helena* is about to depart with the empty stock of an up express in August 1959. (M. S. Stokes)

7) The *Coronation* Class 4-6-2 Pacifics were the mainstay of the Anglo-Scottish expresses for well over thirty years and were fine examples of British express steam locomotives. No 46237 *City of Bristol* gently blows off steam after arriving with an up express on 10th March 1960. To the left is EE Type 4 No D226. (M. Joyce)

8) *Coronation* Class 4-6-2 No 46245 *City of London* shows off its handsome lines whilst standing in the rain at Euston with an express in March 1963. The class was finally rendered extinct in October 1964 and *City of London* was amongst the last survivors. (B. Rands)

9) An onlooker admires the fine outline of *Princess* Class 4-6-2 No 46204 *Princess Louise* at Euston in August 1960 prior to its departure with an express to Liverpool. The *Princess* Class was one of the first to be affected by modernisation and all were withdrawn by November 1962. (G. W. Sharpe)

10) 1B Camden was the main steam depot for Euston and at rest in the yard is *Coronation* Class 4-6-2 No 46222 *Queen Mary* from 66A Polmadie (Glasgow) – 9th August 1962. Camden closed to steam in September 1963 its remaining passenger workings being taken over by 1A Willesden. (T. Wright)

11) The unique BR Class 8P 4-6-2 No 71000 *Duke of Gloucester* is caught by the camera in the shed yard at Camden on 11th September 1956. *Duke of Gloucester* was constructed in 1954, dogged by ill-fortune it spent its short working life at 5A Crewe (North) and was withdrawn from service during November 1962. Preserved at Loughborough. (J. D. Gomersall)

12) *Coronation* Class 4-6-2 No 46239 *City of Chester* at rest inside the gloom of the straight shed at 1B Camden on 9th August 1962. (T. Wright)

13) 1A Willesden shed was situated about five miles from Euston and was a massive complex with a roundhouse and straight shed. It was principally used as a freight depot but had a fair share of passenger workings. This photograph of the yard on 21st February 1965 shows a predominance of small steam types as larger steam locomotives had been banned from working south of Crewe during the summer of 1964. (M. S. Stokes)

14) Class 8F 2-8-0 No 48603 its small tender packed to capacity with coal simmers in the shed yard at Willesden on 27th March 1963. Crewe (North) *Coronation* Class 4-6-2 No 46251 *City of Nottingham* blows off steam behind 48603. (D. K. Jones)

15) Stanier Class 4 2-6-4T No 42611 waits for its next turn of duty in the shed yard at Willesden on 27th October 1963. A large number of these locomotives were allocated here for local passenger and empty stock workings. (Terry Ward)

16) Rebuilt *Jubilee* 4-6-0 No 45736 *Phoenix* is photographed out of steam in the shed yard on 12th October 1963. Its home shed on this date was 12A Carlisle (Kingmoor). Behind *Phoenix* is an unidentified BR Class 2 2-6-0 a number of which were the last steam representatives when Willesden closed to steam in September 1965. (D. K. Jones)

17) *Royal Scot* Class 4-6-0 No 46144 *Honourable Artillery Company* has steam to spare as it wheels a fitted freight through the London suburb of Willesden and heads for Crewe on 12th September 1963. (G. W. Sharpe)

18) Class 8F 2-8-0 No 48628 trundles slowly through the desirable London suburb of South Kenton with an up ballast train on 1st April 1965. The overhead wires and gantry are in position but not yet energised. (W. G. Piggott)

19) *Jubilee* Class 4-6-0 No 45676 *Codrington* stands in the station at Watford Junction with a lengthy empty stock train – cira 1958. To the right of *Codrington* and being admired by two schoolboys is one of the 1947 built Co-Co diesels. (G. W. Sharpe)

20) Class 2P 0-4-4T No 41908 designed for push and pull working shunts at Watford Junction on 4th October 1954. Watford Junction was a change-over point for the St. Albans line. (T. Wright)

21) Watford Junction also boasted a small straight shed coded 1C. Photographed on 8th April 1962 is Class 2 2-6-0 No 46431. The shed was closed in March 1965. (P. Cane)

22) Moving northwards from London our next stop is Tring. *Royal Scot* Class 4-6-0 No 46122 *Royal Ulster Rifleman* storms through with an express made up partly with rather elderly coaches in June 1949. *Royal Ulster Rifleman* is in rebuilt form, with double chimney but not as yet equipped with smoke deflectors. (G. W. Sharpe)

23)	Class 5 4-6-0 No 45375 emerges from the southern portals of Linslade Tunnel with an up parcels train on 17th August 1958. Linslade tunnel was situated a short distance from Leighton Buzzard in the near vicinity of the *Great Train Robbery* of 1963. (K. Barrow)

24)	Bletchley some forty-seven miles from London was an important junction with lines to both Cambridge and Oxford. It also had its own Motive Power Depot coded 1E which closed to steam in July 1965 being replaced by a diesel depot on a different site. On 2nd August 1964 Class 8F 2-8-0 No 48610 simmers gently in the shed yard. (C. P. Stacey)

25) A panoramic and busy view of Bletchley station in September 1958. From left to right – LNW Class 7F 0-8-0 No 48898 draws out of the carriage sheds, *Royal Scot* Class 4-6-0 No 46154 *The Hussar* with a southbound express, a Class 5 4-6-0 on a southbound local, with two Class 4F 0-6-0's, one on a freight and the other one shunting. (K. Barrow)

26) Two *Jubilee* Class 4-6-0's pass each other in Bletchley station on 21st April 1957 – No 45734 *Meteor* with an up stopping train and No 45638 *Zanzibar* with a down express. (K. Barrow)

16

27) We take our leave of Bletchley with a photograph of Class 2P 0-4-4T No 41902 at rest in the station on pilot duties – 29th April 1956. Note the express code headlamps. (G. W. Sharpe)

28) Class 8F 2-8-0 No 48544 heading a train of chalk empties passes Denbigh Hall to the north of Bletchley on 31st August 1964. (C. P. Stacey)

29)   Six miles to the north of Bletchley is Wolverton station. WD Class 8F 2-8-0 No 90329 approaches from the Rugby direction with a special Class 8 freight on 9th April 1964. (K. L. Seal)

30)   *Jubilee* Class 4-6-0 No 45676 *Codrington* in an unkempt state darkens the sky and surrounding countryside with a black smoke-screen as it approaches Wolverton with an up parcels train on the same day. (K. L. Seal)

31) Adjacent to the station is the large carriage and wagon works at Wolverton which for many years had its own allocation of LNWR 0-6-0 Saddle Tanks introduced in 1870 as the Webb version of the Ramsbottom *special tank*. No CD6 rests between duties on 7th August 1957. (J. D. Gomersall)

32) Photographed at Wolverton Works on the same day is sister engine No CD3 in the process of moving some stores wagons. Observe the large LNWR signal post and arm. (J. D. Gomersall)

33) Sixty miles from Euston is Roade and the next four photographs depict the typical types of locomotives and rolling stock in use during 1963 at this busy location. *Royal Scot* Class 4-6-0 No 46140 *The King's Royal Rifle Corps* coasts through Roade Cutting with an up excursion bound for Euston on 25th May 1963. The Northampton line is partly shown in the right foreground. (Terry Ward)

34) Class 6P5F 2-6-0 No 42971 is barely moving with its train of break-vans on 22nd June 1963. Note the small lion and wheel emblem on the tender. (Terry Ward)

35) *Royal Scot* Class 4-6-0 No 46165 *The Ranger (12th London Regt.)* gives a fine impression of power and speed as it roars through Roade with an up express on 13th July 1963. (Terry Ward)

36) Class 5 4-6-0 No 45215 in ex. works condition passes Ashton near Roade with a down fitted freight on 1st June 1963. (Terry Ward)

37) During the electrification of the West Coast Main Line there were many diversions. Whilst work was being carried out between Roade and Rugby many expresses were sent via Northampton. A begrimed *Coronation* Class 4-6-2 No 46256 *Sir William A. Stanier F.R.S.* is south of Northampton with an up express on 17th August 1963. (Terry Ward)

38) An immaculate Rebuilt *Patriot* 4-6-0 No 45530 *Sir Frank Ree* is photographed near to Northampton with an express on 20th May 1964. No 45530 was one of only three members of the class to survive into 1965 the others being Nos 45512/31. (Terry Ward)

39)   Once the pride of Stewarts Lane shed on the Southern Region BR *Britannia* Class 4-6-2 No 70004 *William Shakespeare* is noted in filthy external condition and reduced to a mixed freight duty at Northampton (Kingsthorpe) on 30th May 1964. (Terry Ward)

40)   BR Class 5 (Caprotti) 4-6-0 No 73144 in fine fettle externally starts a mixed freight for the south from Northampton (Spencer Bridge) on 19th May 1964. (Terry Ward)

41)   Between 1947 and 1951 sixty experimental Stanier Class 5 4-6-0's were introduced. No 44744 was one of a batch of such locomotives fitted with Caprotti valve gear which had the disadvantage of making them look ungainly and rather ugly. 44744 is standing in sidings at Northampton (Spencer Bridge) on 6th August 1963. (Terry Ward)

42)   The nearby shed at Northampton had no named passenger locomotives on its books in the late fifties until closure in September 1965. During the period of diversions it therefore played host to many *foreign* passenger engines. Simmering under the coaling plant on 6th October 1963 is a Shrewsbury *Jubilee* Class 4-6-0 No 45699 *Galatea*. (Terry Ward)

43) Rebuilt *Patriot* Class 4-6-0 No 45534 *E. Tootal Broadhurst* is seen at rest in the shed yard at Northampton on 21st July 1963. 45534 was based at 5A Crewe (North) at this date. (Terry Ward)

44) Leeds (Holbeck) Class 5 4-6-0 No 44757 was another of the experimental members of the class. Introduced in 1948 it was equipped with Caprotti valve gear, Timken roller bearings and a double chimney. Photographed under the coaling plant at Northampton on 10th November 1963. (Terry Ward)

45) We rejoin the WCML at Rugby (Midland) a very busy station some eighty-two miles from London and an important junction for Birmingham, Leicester & Leamington to the north and to Northampton & Peterborough to the south. The Leicester and Leamington lines are now closed. BR *Britannia* Class 4-6-2 No 70032 *Tennyson* stands in the station with an express bound for Manchester – circa 1958. (G. W. Sharpe)

46) Class 5 4-6-0 No 44867 in good external condition waits for the road light engine in April 1961. 44867 was a Rugby based engine until July 1961 when it was transferred to Stoke. (C. Hughes)

47) A view of Rugby (Midland) looking northwards from the station towards Crewe during 1965. Visits by steam locomotives had become rare and an unidentified Class 8F 2-8-0 is overshadowed by overhead wires and gantries. To the left are stabled a number of diesel locomotives. (M. P. Smith)

48) Two train-spotters admire *Princess* Class 4-6-2 No 46207 *Princess Arthur of Connaught* from their rather precarious vantage point as the locomotive departs from Rugby (Midland) with a heavy northbound express in August 1961. (G. W. Sharpe)

49) Rebuilt *Jubilee* Class 4-6-0 No 45735 *Comet* makes a spirited departure from Rugby (Midland) with a down excursion in 1963. (G. W. Sharpe)

50) Class 8F 2-8-0 No 48610 passes the station and heads for London with an up freight on a gloomy August day in 1963. To the left of the engine is the coaling plant belonging to 2A Rugby shed and in front of the engine is the ex. Great Central main line. (G. W. Sharpe)

51) Rugby had a large steam shed situated next to the up lines adjacent to the Midland station. In steam in front of the shed are two Class 5 4-6-0's Nos 45256 (8B Warrington) and 45378 (26F Patricroft) – August 1960. The shed closed to steam in May 1965. (H. H. Bleads)

52) *Princess* Class 4-6-2 No 46201 *Princess Elizabeth* is noted dead at the south end of Rugby shed yard, in February 1962. This was in the vicinity of Rugby Testing Station where locomotives were mounted on rollers and performances were noted whilst stationary. (G. W. Sharpe)

53) *Coronation Class* 4-6-2 No 46221 *Queen Elizabeth* lies dead at the south end of Rugby shed yard – circa 1961. In the background is the ex. Great Central Railway main line which passed over the West Coast Main Line via a huge girder bridge known locally as the *birdcage*. (G. W. Sharpe)

54) From Rugby we divert from the WCML to the second city of England – Birmingham. *Royal Scot* Class 4-6-0 No 46168 *The Girl Guide* stands within the confined surroundings of New Street station with a Wolverhampton (High Level) – Euston express on 15th August 1963. During the electrification of the WCML, services to Euston were infrequent and often slow. (D. K. Jones)

55) With its safety valves simmering *Jubilee* Class 4-6-0 No 45688 *Polyphemus* restarts a Wolverhampton (High Level) – Euston express out of New Street in June 1956. Note the short, stubby upper quadrant above the tender. These signals were a prominent feature on the LNW side of the station. (H. H. Bleads)

56) Class 5 4-6-0 No 44876 sets off from New Street with an express bound for Manchester and heads for the lengthy tunnel and long climb to Monument Lane and fresh air in April 1960. (H. H. Bleads)

57) Rebuilt *Patriot* Class 4-6-0 No 45528 blows off a white plume of steam from its safety valves after arriving at New Street with the empty stock of an express to Manchester in April 1957. 45528 was named *R.E.M.E.* in September 1959. (R. Danes)

58) Birmingham (New Street) had three Motive Power Depots which provided locomotives for services to and from this station. Class 5 4-6-0 No 45110 is depicted in the shed yard outside Aston shed on 27th June 1965 some four months before closure. 45110 is preserved on the Severn Valley Railway. (C. P. Stacey)

59) Saltley shed was responsible in the main for freight workings but for a period of time from mid 1961 to mid 1962 had an allocation of *Royal Scot* 4-6-0's for passenger services from the LNW side of Birmingham (New Street). Gathered round the turntable in one of the roundhouses on 26th June 1966 are three 8F 2-8-0's Nos 48538, 48659 and 48101 in company with BR Class 9F 2-10-0 No 92155. Saltley closed to steam in March 1967. (T. Walton)

60) Unrebuilt *Patriot* Class 4-6-0 No 45544 blasts out of the lengthy north tunnel from Birmingham (New Street) and passes Monument Lane shed with an express to Liverpool on 3rd September 1955. Note the wagon ash dampers on the shed road. (J. D. Gomersall)

61) Monument Lane shed was the third depot associated with Birmingham (New Street) and housed a varied selection of locomotive classes. Former Midland Railway, later rebuilt as an LMS Class 3F 0-6-0 No 43187 taking on coal on 3rd September 1955. Monument Lane shed closed to steam in February 1962. (J. D. Gomersall)

62) A panoramic view of Monument Lane shed on a summers day in 1959 showing a variety of motive power – Class 3 2-6-2 Tanks, Class 3F & 4F 0-6-0's, Class 5 4-6-0's, a *Jubilee* Class 4-6-0 and a Class 8F 2-8-0. (R. S. Carpenter)

63) Former Midland Railway (Compound) Class 4P 4-4-0 No 40933 in a siding at Monument Lane shed in July 1957. Monument Lane had the distinction of being the last shed to house these famous locomotives. Nos 40936 and 41168 were in and out of store for years, the latter engine being the last to be condemned in July 1961. (G. W. Sharpe)

64) The last *Jubilee* Class 4-6-0 No 45742 *Connaught* passes the *attractive* Birmingham suburb of Winson Green with a Wolverhampton (High Level) – Euston express, circa 1958. A number of these locomotives were based at Bushbury (Wolverhampton) shed and were the mainstay of these expresses for many years. (R. S. Carpenter)

65) *Jubilee* Class 4-6-0 No 45689 *Ajax* makes hard work of a heavy Birmingham (New Street) to Manchester express in August 1962 as it passes Tipton station which was situated between New Street and Wolverhampton. Tipton was the junction for the Wednesbury and Walsall lines. (L. Brownhill)

66) Former London North Western Class 7F 0-8-0 No 49406 fitted with a tender cab wheezes and creaks its way through Tipton station on a trip freight working in April 1963. A number of these engines were based locally at Bescot shed and some survived until December 1964 but 49406 was withdrawn two months after this picture was taken. (L. Brownhill)

67) Class 5 4-6-0 No 44873 from Bescot shed slowly traverses Tipton curve with a Bescot – Spring Vale mineral train working during 1963. (L. Brownhill)

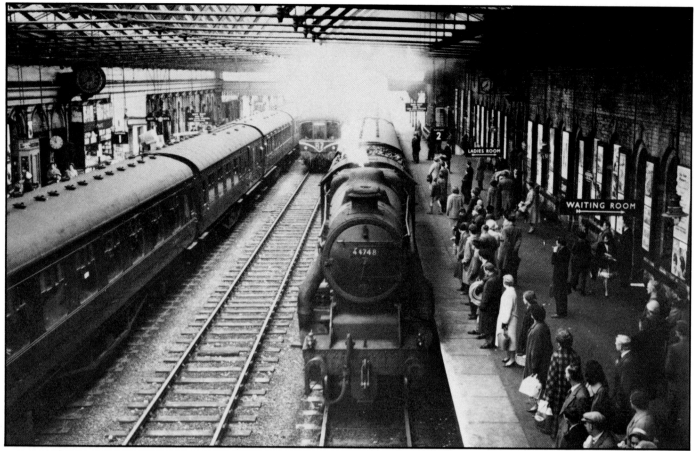

68) Class 5 4-6-0 No 44748 from Longsight shed coasts into Wolverhampton (High Level) station with an express bound for Birmingham (New Street) – July 1961. This locomotive was fitted with Caprotti valve gear and Timken roller bearings. (Michael Paine)

69) A similar view of Wolverhampton (High Level) taken on the same day. An express for the north has almost disappeared out of view and is being followed by a Class 3F *Jinty* 0-6-0 in use as a station pilot. Wolverhampton (High Level) has been completely rebuilt as has Birmingham (New Street). (Michael Paine)

70) Bushbury to the north of Wolverhampton (High Level) was the Motive Power Depot for the area. Photographed in the shed yard in September 1964 is Class 6P5F 4-6-0 No 42957. Bushbury shed closed completely in April 1965. (L. Brownhill)

71) At Stafford we again rejoin the West Coast Main Line some 133 miles to the north of Euston. Stafford boasted its own allocation of steam engines and noted on a murky 29th February 1960 is ex. LNW Class 7F 0-8-0 No 49126 (fitted with tender cab). Stafford shed closed to steam in July 1965. (P. Gardner)

72) *Coronation* Class 4-6-2 No 46254 *City of Stoke-on-Trent* roars through Stafford station and heads for Queensville curve with an up excursion bound for Euston – circa 1960. Stafford was an important junction for Birmingham, Derby and Shrewsbury. (G. W. Sharpe)

73) Stafford station was in the process of being rebuilt on 8th October 1963 when Class 8F 2-8-0 No 48257 was photographed passing under the wires heading for Crewe with a down freight. (B. G. Price)

74) The line between Stafford and Crewe was a well known racing ground and it was between these two locations that *Coronation* Class 4-6-2 No 46220 *Coronation* achieved 114 mph on 29th June 1937. *Royal Scot* Class 4-6-0 No 46140 *The King's Royal Rifle Corps* replenishes its water supply as it passes over Whitmore Troughs on 15th June 1957 whilst in charge of the up *Mancunian*. (R. W. Hinton)

75) Class 5 4-6-0 No 44987 is captured by the camera from a down express as it passes by with an up special bound for Birmingham (New Street) on 15th August 1963 near Madeley. (L. Brownhill)

76) The section between Stafford and Crewe (24 miles) consisted mainly of four tracks and was and still is extremely busy. *Coronation* Class 4-6-2 No 46239 *City of Chester* with accelerator wide open lays a smokescreen over the countryside around Madeley as it storms towards the camera with the up *Royal Scot* from Glasgow-London on 15th May 1957. (N. E. Preedy)

77) *Coronation* Class 4-6-2 No 46243 *City of Lancaster* lends majesty to this rural scene near Madeley in July 1959 as it sweeps around a curve with its extremely heavy load. (Michael Paine)

78) A Burton-on-Trent Class 4F 0-6-0 No 43870 drifts around the curve at Madeley with a train load of pipes in July 1959. (Michael Paine)

79) *Coronation* Class 4-6-2 No 46250 *City of Lichfield* roars through Betley Road with a Perth-Euston express on 19th April 1957. Betley Road was situated between Madeley and Basford. (R. W. Hinton)

80) As we approach Crewe the massive shed complex of 5B Crewe (South) is noted on the left hand side. Crewe (South) was the main provider of locomotives for freight workings. After the passenger shed at 5A Crewe (North) closed to steam the South shed took over its remaining steam workings. This photograph is taken from the London side on 27th August 1967. (R. Picton)

81) The Class 4F 0-6-0's were a common sight around Crewe until 1965/66. No 44405 is by the coaling plant on 23rd June 1962. (G. W. Sharpe)

82)   BR *Britannia* Class 4-6-2 No 70034 *Thomas Hardy* (minus nameplates), its tender filled to capacity waits in a crowded yard at 5B Crewe (South) on 4th April 1967 for the next turn of duty back to its home base of Carlisle. Crewe (South) closed to steam in November 1967. (T. Walton)

83)   The track layout has changed considerably since these pictures of Crewe station were taken. Crewe, the junction for Holyhead, Manchester, Shrewsbury and Stoke was a mecca for spotters and photographers alike. Class 6P5F 2-6-0 No 42981 drifts through the station on avoiding lines with a down horsebox special on 6th September 1963. (G. W. Sharpe)

84) Unrebuilt *Patriot* Class 4-6-0 No 45533 *Lord Rathmore* stands at the north end of Crewe with a stopping train for Liverpool – probably a running in turn. Photographed – circa 1949, note the British Railways emblazoned on the tender. (G. W. Sharpe)

85) *Coronation* Class 4-6-2 No 46228 *Duchess of Rutland* blows out a few jets of steam from the front end as it waits to depart with an up express to Euston – circa 1948. Note the sloping smokebox front and that the locomotive appears to be painted in blue livery. (G. W. Sharpe)

86) The late afternoon sunshine highlights the handsome proportions of *Coronation* Class 4-6-2 No 46230 *Duchess of Buccleuch* as the locomotive draws to a halt with an up express from Glasgow in September 1963. Based at 66A Polmadie (Glasgow) *Duchess of Buccleuch* was to be withdrawn from service two months later. (G. W. Sharpe)

87) *Princess* Class 4-6-2 No 46207 *Princess Arthur of Connaught* takes a through road at Crewe with the heavily loaded up *Merseyside Express* from Liverpool-Euston on 7th July 1952. (R. W. Hinton)

88) *Royal Scot* Class 4-6-0 No 46132 *The King's Regiment Liverpool* threads its way through the masses of tracks and overhead wires on the approach to Crewe from the south at the head of the down *Red Rose* from Euston-Liverpool on 4th July 1959. (R. W. Hinton)

89) A large number of Class 3F 0-6-0 Tanks (Jinties) were allocated to 5B Crewe (South) and were engaged on a multiple of duties e.g. station pilots, shunting and trip freight workings until 1966. No 47494 is engaged on station pilot work on 27th April 1966. (W. G. Piggott)

90) The *premier* shed at Crewe was 5A Crewe (North) which supplied the vast majority of locomotives for the top link workings. *Royal Scot* Class 4-6-0 No 46101 *Royal Scots Grey* is about to leave the shed yard to take up a southbound passenger duty – circa 1957. (G. W. Sharpe)

91) *Coronation* Class 4-6-2 No 46229 *Duchess of Hamilton* is prepared and ready for the road in front of the shed building – circa 1955. Note the sloping smoke-box front and judging by the slack in the tender *Duchess of Hamilton* was due for a rough trip on the down *Mid-Day Scot*. 46229 is now actively preserved. (G. W. Sharpe)

92) Class 2 2-6-2T No 41229 and Class 4 (Fowler) 2-6-4T No 42375 (5F Uttoxeter) stand side by side in the yard, No 42375 is minus a set of driving wheels on 6th September 1961. Crewe (North) consisted of two separate straight sheds and a half-roundhouse. It closed to steam in 1965. (C. Richards)

93) *Coronation* Class 4-6-2 No 46238 *City of Carlisle* in front of the shed at Crewe (North) – circa 1949. Note the unlined black livery, British Railways emblazoned on the tender and the sloping smoke-box front end. *City of Carlisle* appears to be ex. works. (G. W. Sharpe)

94) In addition to the three sheds mentioned Crewe also provided a huge workshop situated adjacent to the main Holyhead line. Apart from being responsible for the construction and maintenance of locomotives it also sadly scrapped them as well. In this picture the last of the *Cauliflowers* or Webb LNWR goods 0-6-0's No 58427 built in 1887 awaits cutting up on 25th March 1956. (J. D. Gomersall)

95) Many types of shunters were allocated to Crewe Works an example of which is an elderly ex. Lancashire & Yorkshire Class 2F 0-6-0T No 51412 which survived until September 1962. Behind the locomotive are a number of spare fireboxes and boilers. Photographed in July 1961. (G. W. Sharpe)

96) A mixture of spotters in standard dress of schoolcaps, scarfs and mackintoshes visit Crewe Works on a winters day in 1959. They are in the main repair shop with a variety of different classes in various stages of overhaul on view. (H. H. Bleads)

97) The unique numbered Class 4F 0-6-0 No 44444 is photographed in Crewe Works yard after repair in September 1954. Note the number 44444 stamped over various parts of the engine, this being a common feature applied to locomotives in all repair shops. (E. A. Elias)

98) Maximum occupation in the main repair shop at Crewe Works on 3rd April 1966 during a guided tour. Two of the engines being overhauled are Class 8F 2-8-0 No 48392 and BR Class 9F 2-10-0 No 92077. This scene was to change rapidly and by February 1967 all repairs to steam locomotives had ceased. (P. Cane)

99) After the lengthy photographic sojourn at Crewe we again move northwards and after crossing the Shropshire Union Canal and the River Weaver we find ourselves at Hartford – twelve miles away from Crewe. *Royal Scot* Class 4-6-0 No 46137 *The Prince of Wales's Volunteers (South Lancashire)* passes through the station with an express for Birmingham, on 31st July 1953. This was the last unrebuilt example of the class. (R. W. Hinton)

100) Two Class 5 4-6-0's Nos 45106 and 45123 deputising for a Pacific head southwards over Acton Grange Viaduct with the up *Royal Scot* on 8th May 1954. Not far from this location is Weaver Junction where trains for Liverpool leave the West Coast Main Line. (R. W. Hinton)

101) *Coronation* Class 4-6-2 No 46235 *City of Birmingham* still with a sloping smoke-box nears Warrington on a misty 8th May 1954 at the head of the heavily loaded down *Mid-Day Scot* from Euston-Glasgow. Note the mixture of upper and lower quadrant signals. *City of Birmingham* is preserved at Birmingham Science Museum. (R. W. Hinton)

102) Class 5 4-6-0 No 45055 in begrimed condition is at Warrington (Bank Quay) station in August 1967 on a goods train. (N. E. Preedy)

103) Another view of Warrington (Bank Quay) station, this time of BR *Britannia* Class 4-6-2 No 70027 *Rising Star* on 6th July 1966. *Rising Star* is in filthy external condition and minus nameplates and is waiting for the road with a down express. (M. P. Smith)

104) To the north of Warrington station was 8B Warrington shed, a large straight depot with a mixed allocation of passenger and freight types. In this photograph of the shed taken on 12th June 1966 there are examples of both LMS & BR engines including BR *Britannia* Class 4-6-2 No 70030 *William Wordsworth*. The shed was rebuilt in 1957 and closed to steam in October 1967. (R. Picton)

105) *Princess* Class 4-6-2 No 46203 *Princess Margaret Rose* looks overdue for a repaint as she speeds through Winwick Quay with a Euston bound express on 2nd January 1956. *Princess Margaret Rose* is preserved at Butterley. (R. W. Hinton)

106) *Jubilee* Class 4-6-0 No 45584 *North West Frontier* on a down express passes BR Class 4 4-6-0 No 75014 on a Manchester train at Winwick on 18th September 1954. Not far from Winwick is the giant Vulcan Engineering Works at Newton-le-Willows. (R. W. Hinton)

107) A few miles to the north of Warrington is the major industrial town of Wigan. Situated to the south of the station was the large steam depot at Springs Branch. Photographed in front of the shed building on 27th August 1967 are a quartet of Class 5 4-6-0's Nos 45321 (left), 44678, 44658 and 45048. (R. Picton)

108) A large number of ex. LNW Class 7F 0-8-0's were allocated to Springs Branch Wigan and some survived there until December 1962. No 49025 is by the coaling plant on 31st March 1962 still active and in steam. It was withdrawn from service in September of the same year. Springs Branch closed to steam in December 1967 being replaced by a diesel depot. (R. Picton)

109) *Coronation* Class 4-6-2 No 46253 *City of St. Albans* drifts through Wigan North Western station with the down *Royal Scot* express from London-Glasgow on 1st October 1955. *City of St. Albans* was one of the first members of the class to be withdrawn from service being condemned in January 1963. (J. D. Gomersall)

110) *Royal Scot* Class 4-6-0 No 46138 *The London Irish Rifleman* departs from Wigan North Western station on 20th September 1958 with a Euston bound express. Note the brazier by the water column, a common sight in steam days for use during the winter months at both stations and steam depots. (R. W. Hinton)

111)   A rather shoddy looking unrebuilt *Patriot* Class 4-6-0 No 45551 ushers its motley collection of three coaches past Standish Junction between Wigan & Preston on 1st May 1954. Of the *Patriot* class a total of ten never carried names, the others being Nos. 45508/10/13/17/42/44/47/49/50. (N. E. Preedy)

112)   Preston had two steam sheds up to September 1961. Lostock Hall was situated off the WCML to the east of Preston station and closed to steam in August 1968. Class 5 4-6-0 No 44942 simmers gently in the shed yard on 12th May 1968. Observe the Anglo-Scottish car carriers rolling stock to the left of the locomotives. (P. B. Hands)

113) Preston, a major town and junction was to be the last large station to play host to steam passenger workings, ending its association with steam in August 1968. Carlisle (Kingmoor) Class 5 4-6-0 No 44677 heads an up freight past Skew Bridge signalbox to the south of Preston station in August 1967. (N. E. Preedy)

114) Class 5 4-6-0 No 45230 and an unidentified *Royal Scot* Class 4-6-0 pass through Preston with the *Mid-Day Scot* on a summers day in 1955. These locomotives would almost certainly be deputising for a failed Pacific. (N. E. Preedy)

115) The driver of Class 5 4-6-0 No 45297 keeps a close watch on his fireman as he is about to climb aboard the tender of the locomotive to top up the water supply prior to departing from Preston with the 11.34am Crewe-Blackpool express on 22nd July 1967. (R. W. Hinton)

116) *Jubilee* Class 4-6-0 No 45705 *Seahorse* stands at Preston during 1963 with an extra passenger train. *Seahorse* a longstanding Blackpool engine was transferred to Newton Heath (Manchester) in June 1964 and withdrawn from service in November 1965. (N. E. Preedy)

117) A group of young trainspotters make a note of the number of Class 2 2-6-0 No 46410 with one breakvan on the outskirts of Preston on 12th April 1963. (R. Picton)

118) Class 5 4-6-0 No 44928 from Bank Hall shed, Liverpool simmers amongst the sunshine and shadows of the confines of Preston station. Photographed on a Rochdale local passenger train on 4th May 1957. (N. E. Preedy)

119) Despite the LMS emblazoned in huge letters on the tender the date of this photograph is 5th August 1967. Class 5 4-6-0 No 45209 is arriving at Preston with a Saturday extra from the north. (N. E. Preedy)

120) Preston shed to the north of the station was subjected to a serious fire in June 1960 involving several locomotives and the shed roof. It survived until September 1961 and was used for a time for the storage of engines. Class 3F 0-6-0T No 47293 is outside the front of the shed in June 1959. (T. Wright)

121) We take our leave of Preston and continue northwards through Oxheys where Class 6P5F 2-6-0 No 42953 is photographed on a down freight. Another memory of the past is the rake of cattle trucks in the background. (R. W. Hinton)

122) On leaving Preston we depart from the industrial belt and head for the scenery of Westmorland and the fells. Unrebuilt *Patriot* Class 4-6-0 No 45543 *Home Guard* passes over Brock Troughs with a Barrow-Euston express on 19th September 1955. *Home Guard* was one of the last two unrebuilt members of the class to survive and along with No 45550 was withdrawn in November 1962. (N. E. Preedy)

123) Twenty-one miles to the north of Preston is Lancaster some 230 miles from Euston. *Jubilee* Class 4-6-0 No 45633 *Aden* arrives at Lancaster (Castle) station with a summer holiday extra during 1955. (N. E. Preedy)

124) Class 5 4-6-0 No 45435 from Carnforth shed entertains a youthful audience at Lancaster (Castle) station before departing to Manchester with an express from Heysham on 22nd July 1967. (R. W. Hinton)

125) BR *Britannia* Class 4-6-2 No 70011 *Hotspur* (its name painted on the smoke deflector) passes through Lancaster with a southbound goods on 22nd July 1967. (N. E. Preedy)

126) Some distance away from Lancaster (Castle) and on a separate line was the steam shed at Green Ayre. An elderly Class 2P 4-4-0 No 40362 is about to depart from the shed yard in the early 1950's. (G. W. Sharpe)

127) *Jubilee* Class 4-6-0 No 45567 *South Australia* sweeps through Hest Bank on the shores of Morecambe Bay with a down fitted freight train in 1960. (N. E. Preedy)

128) The last active BR *Britannia* Class 4-6-2 No 70013 *Oliver Cromwell* departs from Carnforth with a Locomotive Club of Great Britain enthusiasts special on 16th June 1968. *Oliver Cromwell* is preserved at Bressingham. (N. E. Preedy)

129) Carnforth shed was one of the last three depots on British Railways to house steam engines, the others being Lostock Hall (Preston) & Rose Grove (Burnley). Leeds (Holbeck) *Jubilee* Class 4-6-0 No 45593 *Kolhapur* is being prepared for special service in the shed yard in 1966. *Kolhapur* is preserved at Tyseley. (B. J. Miller)

130) Class 5 4-6-0 No 44897 and BR Class 5 4-6-0 No 92016 both in steam are tender to tender in the yard at Carnforth on 26th August 1967. The shed closed to steam in August 1968 and is now used as a live steam museum complete with a working coaling plant. (R. Picton)

131) The driver of *Jubilee* Class 4-6-0 No 45599 *Bechuanaland* waves to the camera as his charge thunders through Milnthorpe with a Glasgow-Manchester express on 10th September 1956. (N. E. Preedy)

132) Class 6P5F 2-6-0 No 42947 its tender rail almost overflowing with coal accepts a drink from Dillicar Troughs in the Lune Valley and has steam to spare in charge of a freight on 31st July 1959. The hills around Dillicar almost overcome the locomotive and train. (N. E. Preedy)

133) Tebay, in the middle of nowhere and 262 miles from Euston became famous due to it being located at the start of the notorious incline of Shap. A shed was located a short distance to the south of the station and provided locomotives to assist trains to Shap summit. Class 4 2-6-4T No 42154 rests between such duties in the shed yard on 12th May 1966. (N. E. Preedy)

134) Class 4 2-6-0 No 43009 and Class 4 (Fowler) 2-6-4T No 42414 stand in an almost deserted shed yard on 22nd September 1962. Tebay shed closed at the end of 1967 and there is little evidence of the station and shed today. (R. Picton)

135) Tebay is the scene for the stop-over of *Coronation* Class 4-6-2 No 46251 *City of Nottingham* on an S.L.S. tour from Birmingham-Carlisle on 12th July 1964. In less than three months the once common sight of these majestic locomotives on the West Coast Main Line was lost forever. (N. E. Preedy)

136) BR *Britannia* Class 4-6-2 No 70042 *Lord Roberts* (minus nameplates) rushes through Tebay station with a short southbound fitted freight on 12th May 1966. Sister engine No 70008 *Black Prince* commences the ascent to Shap Summit with an equally short fitted freight. The line branching off to the right used to go to Darlington. (N. E. Preedy)

137) A Carlisle (Upperby) Class 5 4-6-0 No 44937 commences the long climb of almost eight miles to Shap summit, the last four miles being 1 in 75 at the head of a train of parcel vans without the aid of rear end assistance on 12th May 1965. (N. E. Preedy)

138) Class 4 (Stanier) 2-6-4T No 42232 lends a hand by giving rear end assistance to a northbound freight shortly after leaving Tebay on 12th May 1965. (N. E. Preedy)

139) The Stanier beat echoes from the cutting being passed by Class 5 4-6-0 No 44692 on the climb to Shap summit on 12th May 1965. (N. E. Preedy)

140) *Royal Scot* Class 4-6-0 No 46118 *Royal Welch Fusilier* approaches Scout Green signalbox on the climb to Shap summit in 1960 with a down express. (B. J. Miller)

141) Class 5 4-6-0 No 45120 from Carlisle (Kingmoor) passes the bleak outpost of Gresholm on the climb to Shap – 10th May 1966. (N. E. Preedy)

142) *Royal Scot* Class 4-6-0 No 46105 *Cameron Highlander* a Scottish representative of this famous class attacks Shap on 22nd September 1962 with the 10.57am Lancaster-Carlisle express. By the end of 1962 all of the Scottish examples had been withdrawn. (R. Picton)

143) Shap Summit is reached some 916 feet above sea level and the signalbox is the subject of this photograph on 25th July 1954. From here there is a long downhill run to Carlisle in excess of thirty miles giving relief to the locomotives and crew. (R. W. Hinton)

144) A number of passengers admire *Royal Scot* Class 4-6-0 No 46106 *Gordon Highlander* as it draws to a halt in Penrith station with an empty stock train on 25th July 1954. *Gordon Highlander* was unique in the fact that it was equipped with different smoke deflectors to the rest of the class. (R. W. Hinton)

145) Without its nameplates but still a fine looking locomotive BR *Britannia* Class 4-6-2 No 70029 *Shooting Star* drifts along light engine near to Carlisle (Upperby) in late 1965. (D. K. Jones)

146) By the time this photograph was taken on 15th May 1966 the more famous representatives of the LMS had long since been withdrawn. Carlisle (Upperby) shed plays host to Class 5 4-6-0 No 45182 from Barrow. (D. Titheridge)

147) Class 2 2-6-2T No 41207 and Class 2 2-6-0 No 46455 are dead in the shed yard at Carlisle (Upperby) on the same day. Despite its stored appearance 46455 was not withdrawn. Upperby shed to the south of Carlisle station closed to steam in December 1966. (D. Titheridge)

148) Safety valve simmering, injector on and blower open, a typical *right away* as *Jubilee* Class 4-6-0 No 45689 *Ajax* builds up speed on the outskirts of Carlisle with a southbound express on 20th March 1960. The line from Leeds passes under the two tracks on the right of the picture. (D. K. Jones)

149) Carlisle Citadel station lies 299 miles from Euston via the WCML. This scene taken on 27th September 1962 gives a false picture of Citadel being a quiet station, it was far from it. This panoramic view of the south end of the station concentrates on the intricate cross-overs. On the left simmering in a bay platform is Class 2 2-6-0 No 46458 with two coaches. (R. Picton)

150) A busy scene at Carlisle Citadel. *Coronation* Class 4-6-2 No 46241 *City of Edinburgh* (with sloping smoke-box) a Camden engine awaits the arrival of a southbound Friday afternoon express, where locos will be changed. The date 1st July 1955 – the time 16.00hrs. An LNER B1 Class 4-6-0 No 61100 helps complete the picture. (J. D. Gomersall)

151) For many years the *Jinty* Class 3F 0-6-0 Tanks were ever present at Citadel station on pilot duties until 1966. This picture of a clean No 47288 engaged on such a duty was taken on 1st April 1964. (G. W. Sharpe)

152) Another *Jinty* Class 3F 0-6-0T No 47515 is photographed shunting empty stock at the north end of the station, this time on 13th August 1962. (B. G. Price)

153) With the driver of the Carlisle station pilot Class 3F 0-6-0T No 47292 looking on, *Princess* Class 4-6-2 No 46204 *Princess Louise* takes a breather before departing to the south with a heavy express on 11th February 1961. Carlisle was the junction for Edinburgh, Silloth, Maryport, Leeds and Newcastle. (D. K. Jones)

154) The next two photographs are taken from a vantage point near to Etterby Bridge which is to the north of Citadel station and crosses the River Eden. Class 5 4-6-0 No 44809 departs from Kingmoor yard with a southbound freight on 23rd August 1967. To the left a new diesel depot is being constructed to replace the steam shed on the right. (N. E. Preedy)

155) BR *Britannia* Class 4-6-2 No 70031 *Byron* stripped of nameplates crosses Etterby Bridge with a rather insulting load consisting of just two wagons and a breakvan on 17th June 1967. (N. E. Preedy)

156) Carlisle (Kingmoor) shed was a massive straight depot with an allocation in excess of three figures for many years and was a mecca for spotters. BR *Britannia* Class 4-6-2 No 70032 *Tennyson* (without nameplates) and an unidentified Class 5 4-6-0 are seen at rest outside the south end of the shed on 23rd July 1966. (B. J. Miller)

157) The front end of Class 4 2-6-4T (Fowler) No 42369 and the begrimed shed building are lit up by early morning sunshine on 20th October 1963. In the background is BR *Clan* Class 4-6-2 No 72005 *Clan Macgregor* and *Royal Scot* Class 4-6-0 No 46132 *The King's Regiment Liverpool*. (R. Hennefer)

158) *Jubilee* Class 4-6-0 No 45580 *Burma* stands in a packed yard at the north end of Kingmoor shed on 17th August 1952. Observe the huge concrete coaling plant in the background. (N. E. Preedy)

159) Polmadie (Glasgow) *Coronation* Class 4-6-2 No 46231 *Duchess of Atholl* in immaculate condition awaits a turn of duty with the *Royal Scot* during 1955. (N. E. Preedy)

160) Ex. Caledonian Railway Class 3F 0-6-0 No 57653 is surrounded by a haze of steam and smoke at the north end of Kingmoor yard on 29th August 1957. This locomotive was withdrawn in January 1961 but was stored at Kingmoor from 1959-1963. Kingmoor shed closed completely on 1st January 1968. (T. Wright)

161) The third major shed at Carlisle is Canal which was situated on the Carlisle-Edinburgh line and serviced the ex. LNER locomotives used on this route until closure in August 1963. LNER K1 Class 2-6-0 No 62028 from 52C Blaydon simmers gently outside the gloomy interior of the shed on 28th August 1957. (J. D. Gomersall)

162) We take our leave of Carlisle and cross the Scottish border passing long forgotten stations like Ecclefechan and Nethercleugh and arrive at Beattock, where a steam shed provided banking engines for trains climbing the arduous ten miles of Beattock bank. Class 4 2-6-4T No 42693 lies idle at the side of the shed on 31st July 1966. (R. Picton)

163) Ex. Caledonian Railway Class 2P 0-4-4T No 55261 shunts wagons at Carstairs, 372 miles north of London. Carstairs still is a junction for Edinburgh and used to have its own depot at the south end of the station which closed to steam in March 1967. The photograph of 55261 was taken during 1955. (N. E. Preedy)

164) Stark simplicity, and rugged with it, was the hallmark of the ex. CR *Jumbo* 2F 0-6-0's built from 1883 onwards. This is No 57237, the very first one and still banging about alongside the WCML near Wishaw in 1962 with about two million miles on the clock. Despite the new wooden doors on the cab and looking good for another million miles 57237 was withdrawn before the year was out. (Peter Hay)

165) Ex. CR Class 2F 0-6-0 No 57299 makes haste to clear the WCML at Shields Colliery signalbox with its load of goods wagons in 1962. The wagons are typical of the area and its traffic: empty coal: a load of moulding sand and a bogie wagon of steel plate. Clayton Type 1 diesels were about to replace these engines though *they* did not last 70 years. (Peter Hay)

166) BR *Britannia* Class 4-6-2 No 70048 *The Territorial Army 1908-1958* heading south through Flemington with an Anglo-Scottish express on 2nd May 1960. An unexpected distant signal at danger has caught the fireman in the middle of a heavy round of firing and closing the regulator has produced thick smoke. The goods line signals on the right are Caledonian Railway. (Peter Hay)

167) 66B Motherwell shed was situated just to the East of the WCML on the line to Coatbridge. Sited in a heavy industry area most of its workings were freight. This panoramic view of the shed taken in 1962 shows a selection of classes in the yard including shed pilot ex. CR Class 3F 0-6-0T No 56338. Motherwell closed to steam in May 1967. (Peter Hay)

168) Some typical Motherwell scenery in 1960 containing a selection of colliery tips, a bogie bolster wagon loaded with girders for Argentina and an ex. CR Class 0F 0-4-0ST No 56031 equipped with a stovepipe chimney. The front and rear buffers are made of thick timber baulks faced with iron as was the buffer of its coal cart tender. (Peter Hay)

169) This photograph taken on 18th June 1962 is an extremely rare one of an ex. Caledonian Railway Class 3P 4-4-0 No 54465 at work under the wires at Motherwell. By this date only a handful were still in service, very few of them active. 54465 was withdrawn four months later. (G. S. Birtwell)

170) The WCML platforms at Motherwell in 1959 before the wires came still presented a typical appearance for that part of the Scottish lowlands: smoke blackened with lots of stone and hard wearing pavement. An ex. CR *Jumbo* Class 2F 0-6-0 No 57377 travels tender-first through the station with a short coal train from one of the many local pits. (Peter Hay)

171) A standard CR Class 3F 0-6-0 Tank No 56295 with a short coal train nears Rutherglen in 1957. The up WCML is in the foreground, while in the background this train's customers probe the skyline with their chimneys. (Peter Hay)

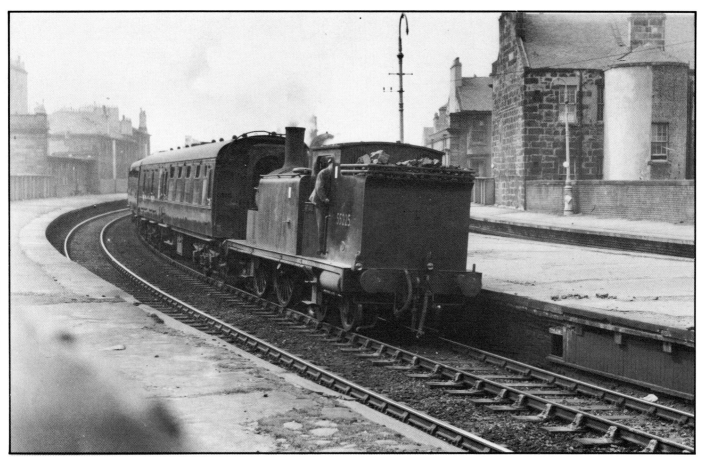

172) Eglington Street was the last station on the WCML before Glasgow (Central). Once busy with local passengers, Eglington Street itself closed in 1965 and when this picture was taken in 1960 it was clearly in a state of decay. Hurrying through with the empty stock of a recently arrived express is ex. CR Class 2P 0-4-4T No 55225. (Peter Hay)

173) By Eglington Street station was the shed for Glasgow (Central) 66A Polmadie, a large complex with an equally large allocation. On show in the shed yard is BR *Britannia* Class 4-6-2 No 70052 *Firth of Tay* on 17th March 1955. Five of these engines Nos 70050-54 were based here until October 1958. (N. E. Preedy)

174) Polmadie had a batch of *Coronation* Class 4-6-2's allocated for many years and they had a major share in top-link workings like the *Royal Scot* and *Mid-Day Scot*. One of the Polmadie *Coronations* No 46222 *Queen Mary* (with sloping smokebox) bathed in sunshine shares the shed yard with Class 4 2-6-4T No 42240 on 17th March 1952. (N. E. Preedy)

175) Also based at 66A Polmadie was a batch of BR *Clan* Class 4-6-2's Nos 72000-4. Not very popular engines all five were withdrawn in December 1962. No 72002 *Clan Campbell* replenishes its water supply in the shed yard in March 1952. Polmadie closed to steam in May 1967 and has since been demolished. (R. W. Hinton)

176) This is a magnificent picture of what it was all about before the diesels arrived. A Camden based *Coronation* Class 4-6-2 No 46236 *City of Bradford* in immaculate external condition and with headboard in place prepares to depart from Glasgow (Central) for the long journey south with the up *Royal Scot* in 1957. (N. E. Preedy)

177) A fine gantry of Caledonian Railway signals on the outskirts of Glasgow (Central) which probably date from the great rebuilding of the Clyde River bridges and Central station during the early part of this century. The signals for the up lines are elevated on lattice posts so that they can be seen over the top of the viaduct carrying the ex. G & SWR lines into St. Enoch. (Peter Hay)

178) Ex. Caledonian Railway Class 2P 0-4-4T No 55220 arrives at Glasgow (Central) with a local non corridor stock passenger train from the Glasgow suburbs in 1957. This was a typical everyday scene until the end of the 1950's. (N. E. Preedy)

179) Ex. CR Class 2P 0-4-4T No 55265 was one of the newest of its type being of a slightly enlarged design built for the LMS in 1925. It is seen here as a station pilot at Glasgow (Central) in 1952 its shedplate in an unusual position. The main line arrival platforms are under the elaborate glass roof in the background to the left. (Peter Hay)

180) In immaculate black livery and with British Railways emblazoned on its side tanks Class 4 (Fowler) 2-6-4T No 42420 accelerates out of Glasgow (Central) with a suburban train consisting of non corridor stock to Gourock in about 1950. (N. E. Preedy)

181) We take our leave of Glasgow (Central) – 401 miles from London (Euston) with this fine picture of the *Royal Scot* carriage headboard on 25th June 1956. Steam has long since vanished from this fine old station but no doubt the ghosts of the *Caledonian* and *Coronation* locomotives still linger on inside its cavernous interior. (J. D. Gomersall)